SITA'S ABDUCTION

RAMA'S QUEST TO RESCUE

KONDA MURALI

ISBN 979-888569263-2

I dedicate the book to myself as I always keep motivate myself irrespective of praises and rewards. I also dedicate this book to my family and friends, without them, I would not have completed the book.

Contents

Foreword

I am very happy to associate with Konda Murali in CVR college of engineering. The beauty of his personality is his simplicity. I was surprised to look at his interest in writing. And I was so thrilled to see him as a young writer who completed thirteen books of different genres. Retelling the Ramayan in simple English to spread the message of it to the world is an amazing thing. I hope that he difinitely would reach the pinnacle position in writing career.

Singathi Upendar
PGT English
Social Welfare Residential School
Asifabad

Preface

I feel, I am very fortunate to retell the Ramayan. To utter the word, Rama, people feel very blessed but I got the opportunity to read and retell the Ramayan in simple English. The devotion in me helped to complete the book. It is true that the story itself searches for its writer. In this regard, the story might have chosen me to disseminate its message.

Konda Murali
Cell no: 9441431090
Mail ID: mahabhi1310@gmail.com

Acknowledgements

I would like to acknowledge to my family members, friends and colleagues for encouraging me to write and to grow as a passionate author and poet.

Prologue

During the exile of Rama, Laxmana and Sita, they travel through Dandakaranya. From there they reach Panchavati which is near to present Bhadrachalam. There Laxmana builds Parnasala for them. Meanwhile untoward incidents take place.

A rakshasi woman, Surpanakha, the sister of Ravana, was captivated by the matchless beauty of Sri Rama. She attempted to seduce him. But when she failed to win either of the two princes, she turned to attackMother Sita. Lakshmana cut off her nose and ears as a punishment. Hearing of this, her demon brother, Khara, organized an attack against the princes. Sri Rama destroyed Khara and his huge army.

In order to avenge her humiliation, Surpanakha approached Ravana. She well knew of his weakness for women, and the wily demoness described the bewitching beauty of Mother Sita. Her intention to bring this beautiful woman to him was foiled and she was mutilated. Ravana was aroused more by lust than by anger and he resolved to punish Sri Rama by capturing Mother Sita.

Ravana elicited the aid of Maricha who assumed the form of a golden deer and enticed Mother Sita. Entranced by the beauty of the deer, she pleaded with Sri Rama to get her the deer. Leaving Mother Sita under Lakshmana's guard, he endlessly chased the deer. Unable to capture the deer, he shot a fatal arrow at it. With his last breath, Maricha called out the name of Lakshmana in the voice of Sri Rama. When Mother Sita heard the cry, she was afraid that his life was in danger. She insisted that Lakshmana rush to his aid. Lakshmana tried to assure her that Sri Rama was invincible, and that it was best if he obeyed Sri Rama's orders to protect her. On the verge of hysterics, Mother Sita insisted that it was not she but her lord who needed Lakshmana's help. After drawing a protective circle round the cottage, he stipulated that she was not to go outside the circle.

When Ravana found her alone and unprotected, he appeared in the guise of an ascetic requesting Mother Sita's hospitality. Unaware of his devious plan, Mother Sita left the protection of the circle, and was then forcibly carried away by Ravana. Jatayu, a giant vulture and friend of Sri Rama, tried to rescue Mother Sita, but was mortally wounded. Mother Sita kept her presence of mind, and dropped her jewels among some monkeys.

When Ravana reached Lanka, he kept her under guard in the Asoka Garden. Ravana used various means of persuasion to force her to accept him. Of course, Mother Sita was eternally devoted to Sri Rama and rebuffed his overtures.

Sri Rama and Lakshmana learnt about Mother Sita's abduction from Jatayu. Because of his devotion and service to Sri Rama, Jatayu received liberation from Sri Rama. The princes immediately set out in search of Mother Sita. During their quest, Sri Rama killed a demon Kabandha, thus liberating him from a curse. They also met the ascetic Shabari, who directed them towards Rsymukha Hill where they would meet Sugreeva and Hanuman.

CHAPTER ONE

After Bharatha and Shathrugna had gone back to Ayodhya, Rama, Laxmana and Sita entered the dreadful forest, named Dandakaranya. After walking for few days in the forest, they found Tapasula Ashram. The ashram was more beautiful than the previous'. They found different kinds of animals, trees and birds which they had never seen before. The ashram was like the house of Brahma. The hermits in it were chanting mantras and it echoed with positive sanctity. When they entered the ashram, the hermits were so happy to see Rama, Laxmana and Sita in their ashram. The hermits saw them for a while without blinking their eyes.

They received the hermits' hospitality with grandeur. Later the hermits felicitated Rama, Laxmana and Sita as they were equal to gods to them. They provided fruits, stems, water and the others to eat. They told Rama that he was the great person who had popularity over the world. They knew him to a humble man, who always stands on the righteousness and truth. They said that it was their duty to protect him as well as Laxmana and Sita. They stated, he was their king and god irrespective of his place if it was a forest or city.

Rama, Laxmana and Sita spent that night in Tapasula ashram and started their journey in the early morning. On their way, they crossed the mount of Suryodaya. They entered the dense forest which had a lot of tigers and bears.

There was no sign of any lakes and rivers in it. The dreadful voices of crickets and birds were heard.

Suddenly they encountered a giant man who was looking like the hill. His eyes were deep and the big mouth. His tremble appearance made them frightened. He wore the skin of tiger and wore the skulls as if it was garland. On seeing Rama, Laxmana and Sita, he was running towards them. Sita was afraid of looking at his giant, terrible figure.

He was shouting at Rama, Laxmana and Sita. He asked them who they were. Why they were roaming in the forest with a lady. He told then that he was Viradha. He also said that he was living in the forest hunting the animals and eating their meat. He looked at Sita and admired her beauty. He asked Rama to give her to him. Otherwise he would kill Rama and Laxmana. When Sita heard that she was rattled with his words.

Later Rama told Viradha everything, why they had to roam in the forest along with his wife and brother. Laxmana was interfered their conversation and asked his brother why he had to make conversation with the giant instead of killing him. Laxmana asked permission to kill him with his powerful arrow.

Then Viradha, the giant man interrupted Rama and Laxmana's conversation. He roared at them and asked why they were making mess while he was speaking. Rama asked him who he was and how dare to speaking to them in a rude manner. Then the giant man told that he was son of Shathahrada. All the raakshasas call me Viradha in this forest. He told that he had done the great penance, for that Lord Brahma appeared and gave me a boon. The boon was that no one would kill me.

So Viradha ordered Rama to leave Sita and went back otherwise he would kill them. When Rama heard that, he raged on the giant. Rama's eyes turned into red for speaking so. Then he said to the giant, "You are an evil giant. How dare you to speak like that? You are looking for your death. I will definitely kill you in the war" Rama immediately took his arrow from his quiver and shot at the giant. Then the arrow was split into seven and they pierced into his body. With that his body was torn and blood started coming out like a flow. He immediately fell onto the ground.

After some time the giant again woke up from the ground as the arrows hurt him little though the blood poured. When he woke up, the two brothers again started shooting arrows at him. He defended all of the arrows with his shula. He later threw his powerful shula at the brothers. Then Rama defended with his arrows. The arrows broke the shula into two pieces. Then Rama and Laxmana took their swords and pierced into his body. Though he was in pain, he lifted Rama and Laxmana onto his arms.

Then Rama told Laxmana let him carry us on his shoulders. Sita cried looking at Rama and Laxmana. She pleaded the giant not to kill them. Without them I will not exist. Tigers may kill me, said Sita. Rama worried looking at Sita. He immediately broke his two arms with his devine strength. With that he again fell onto the ground but he was alive.

Then Rama told Laxmana, "As long as he was on the earth, he will not be killed. So it is better to bury him" Later Laxmana had dug deep and wide pit. Meanwhile Rama had set his foot on the giant's throat. Then Viradha came to know the power of Rama. Then he realized and said that he couldn't identify his strength. He stated that Rama had the equal strength of Lord Indra.

Then Viradha told his story. He told them that he was killed by Tumbura and cursed by Kubera. Kubera cursed me to live as Rakshasa until you will kill me. Today I was killed and I am very happy today for becoming Gandharva again which was my previous birth. He thanked Rama and Laxmana for ending his curse as Rakshasa. Then Rama kicked on his throat. Simultaneously Rakshasa's life turned into Gandharva. Later he went to paradise. The dead body was buried later.

Rama after killing the giant, hugged Sita and he said to her that the forest was very dangerous. Though it was very tough to live in the forest for us, it was inevitable. After few hours of journey in the forest, they reached Sarabhanga Maharshi. There they saw a wonder. There was a chariot in the ashram. It was shining like the sun and it was in the sky. It was flying in the air. They wondered how the heavy chariot was flying in the air without touching the ground. The green horses were tethered to it. There they also found a white umbrella. It was exactly looking like the moon.

And it was shining with the wonderful flower garlands. There the maids were creating air flow with the handmade fans and the gandharvas were roaming around them. Many hermits were chanting the mantras from Vedas in the sky. Lord Indra was speaking to Sarabangha Maharshi. Rama felt very happy to Lord Indra.

Rama told Laxmana and Sita that they should wait there.

He would go towards the place to talk to Lord Indra. Lord Indra saw Rama from a distance and with the permission of Sarabangha Maharshi, Lord Indra allowed Rama into the chariot. Lord spoke to Rama and enquired their wellness. Indra told Sarabangha Maharshi that he would help Rama and he flew to the paradise. After Indra had flown, Sarabangha Maharshi came to the place where Sita and Laxmana were waiting along with Rama. They touched his feet and took his blessings and later he invited them into his ashram.

Rama asked Maharshi why Lord Indra had come there. Then Maharshi told that he had satisfied with my penance. So he blessed me with a boon. Indra also promised me that he would take me to the heaven. But your arrival made my journey cancel. I will go after giving you hospitality, said Sarabangha Maharshi.

Later Rama enquired about the place. Then Maharshi told Suthiksha was living here. He would accompany you in everything. Now it is the time for me, I left the heaven. You cross the river Mandakini, there you will find Suthiksha, said Sarabangha Maharshi. Meanwhile Sarabangha Maharshi turned into light form and his physical body disappeared and the light flew to the heaven.

After Sarabangha had gone to the heaven, many hermits came to see Rama. They praised Rama and his dynasty. They said that they had heard the greatness of him. They told him that the king who treat his people as if they were his sons, he would reach the heaven. There he was also adored with fruits and stems. The king who torture his people with a lot of taxes, he would reach the hell and be punished.

They pleaded Rama to save the brahmans those who were in Vanaprastha. Many of them were being killed brutally by raakshasas on the bank of Mandakini. They also said that they were unable to rescue those who were doing meditation. So we request you to save them, said the hermits.

Then Rama replied to them in this way, "You shouldn't request me. It is my duty to save them. The god gave me an opportunity to protect them. I knew, my exile also was useful to many. I will definitely kill all of the raakshasas" Rama promised them and told to go to Suthiksha Maharshi.

They later started for the ashram of Suthikshna. They crossed many beautiful places and rivers on the way to the ashram. The forest was filled different species of trees and animals. They finally reached the ashram after few hours of their journey on walk. Suthikshna, who was with long twisted hair, welcomed Rama, Laxmana and Sita. Rama introduced himself and he introduced his wife and brother. Rama also said that he had come to see him. Then Suthikshna felt very happy and embraced him.

Suthikshna told, "Rama! You are the man of righteousness. I am very happy to see you in my ashram. I was waiting for a long time. I pity on your situation. Even Indra did not escape from the troubles like you" So make the exile useful and be happy with Sita and Laxmana.

CHAPTER TWO

Rama replied, "Maharshi! I was looking for a shelter in this forest. Sarabangha Maharshi told about you. With his advice of him, I came here"

Then Suthikshna said, "This ashram is so beautiful. Many priests and hermits are living here. You can find multi fruits and stems. This is safe place to live in. Here violence of animals and humans are prohibited"

Rama replied that they were not going to live there permanently. They would spend only one night. Then Suthikshna said, "Okay" Rama, Laxmana and Sita spent happily in the ashram that night.

Next morning Rama, Laxmana and Sita met Suthikshna. They thanked him for giving accommodation to them in his ashram. They asked his permission to move further. When he asked to stay back for some time, Rama replied that they had to start before the sun shone. When the hermit gave them permission, they took his blessings.

Then they again started their journey. They were proceeding enjoying the beauty of nature. They were also enjoying the taste of fruits on the way. They found many lakes, tanks, ponds, brooks, waterfalls and rivers. They were enjoying birds' singing peacocks' dancing. Thus their journey was wonderful.

There they spent that night. Rama woke up in the early morning and did his morning routine. Later Rama, Laxmana and Sita decided to leave the place so they went to Suthikshna and told him that they were leaving the place. They said that they had come to him to take his permission. He gave them permission to go. Later they took his blessings and was about to start.

Then Suthikshna gave them some suggestions and directions. He advised them to protect themselves from cruel animals and weather. He also suggested them to enjoy beauty of the forest. Then Rama said, "Okay" They later moved into the forest. While they were traveling, Sita told Rama how the society was filled with evils. Sita praised her husband's qualities. She felt her husband was the best man in the world. She knew the men in the society were with full of lust.

Then Rama replied that it was his duty to protect the righteousness. So many hermits are suffering from raakshasas in this forest. All are waiting for someone who will protect them. So it is the duty of me to protect them. When they reached a place, all the hermits were very happy to see Rama. They felt that they are going to be saved by him. Then Rama promised them at any situation, he would not be going to leave his promise. To save them, he was ready to forgo Sita and Laxmana but he wouldn't live without saving them.

The hermits gave accommodation to Rama, Sita and Laxmana. They took rest in the ashram that night. The next they woke up in the early morning. Rama and Laxmana went to the lake to take bath. When they about to dip in the lake, the noise was heard. They looked the surroundings to know where the voice was coming from but they didn't see anyone. Then they went the hermit named Dharmabrutha and asked him eagerly about the strange noise in the lake.

Then the hermit told him that it was the lake, Panchapsara. Here the hermit, Mandakarni had performed a great penance. Then lord Indra sent his five beautiful angels to him. They married the hermit, Mandakarni. Then the hermit constructed a beautiful house beneath the lake. They there sometimes dance. The hermit said to Rama, "It might be the sound made by them" Then Rama was surprised to listen to that. Later they took bath in the lake and performed their morning puja.

Thus, Rama, Sita and Laxmana were spending different ashrams and spending their time in the forest. Thus their ten years of forest life was completed. Later they came back to the ashram of Suthikshna, seeing different locations. They asked Suthikshna about Agasthya. Then Suthikshna told them about Agasthya. He suggested them to visit the brother of Agasthya. "Later he will tell you about his brother" said Suthikshna.

Next they started to the ashram of Agasthya's brother. They reached the ashram and took his blessings. That evening they were accommodated in the ashram and in the night they were provided fruits and stems. That night they knew the way to the ashram of Agasthya. In early morning after taking bath, they started to the ashram of Agasthya.

Laxmana went to Agasthya and told him in this way, "I am Laxmana. My brother Rama and his wife Sita are waiting outside. We are the sons of the king, Dasharatha. We came from Ayodhya. We are living in the forest as a part of exile of fourteen years" Then the hermit, Agasthya felt very happy on Rama's arrival to his ashram. Even he had been waiting for his arrival for a long time. He told Laxmana to bring Rama and Sita in. It is not good for me to keep Rama waiting. Them Laxmana went back and brought Rama and Sita before Agasthya.

When Agasthya saw Rama and Sita, his heart felt thrilled. He felt as if he is looking lord Vishnu and Laxmi. Later Agasthya adored Rama along with his people in the ashram. He also provide them fresh fruits and stems. After they received hospitality from Agasthya, Rama was told about the bow of Vishnu. Agasthya told, "With this bow, I killed so many raakshasas. It is the most powerful weapon. So now I want to present It to you so that you can use it wherever necessary. If it is used by you, no one can encounter you at the war"

Agasthya felt very happy for the sojourn of Rama, Laxmana and Sita. "Your departure is making me sad and I am worried mostly about Sita. She did not face any difficulties from her childhood. Now she is sauntering in the forest facing lot of troubles. I suggest you to take care of her otherwise she will be afraid of the cruel animals" said Agasthya.

Then Rama replied that he would definitely take care of her. He told that in fact it was his duty to look after her. Later Rama was known about the beautiful place called Panchavati. Agasthya suggested Rama to build a hut there and start living in it as it was the best place in the forest to live in. Agasthya was very happy with Rama's obedience. He said that he had not seen such kind of person in the world. Rama, Laxmana and Sita took blessings of Agasthya later they started towards Panchavati. They were surprised to look at the beautiful places and birds on their way to Panchavati.

Before they reach Panchavati, Rama and Laxmana had come across a big eagle named Jatayu. They thought that it might be a kind of giant. Then the eagle melodiously told them that it was their father's friend. Then Rama and Laxmana felt very happy to hear their father's name from the eagle. Rama had a suspicious on it and enquired it about their dynasty. Then Jatayu started explaining their dynasty details.

It said whole history of their dynasty which made Rama and Laxmana astonished. They later knew Jatayu was their friend and not an enemy. Jatayu promised them that it was its duty to take care of Sita. Then Rama and Laxmana had a complete belief on it.

Rama showed Panchavati to Laxmana and Sita. He suggested Laxmana to search for a better place to build Parnashala. Then Laxmana watched the surroundings and decided to build Parnashala where the multicolored flowers are grown. Just beside the place there is the river Godavari. Even Agasthya told them about the place. Different species of birds and animals were also found there.

So Laxmana built beautiful Parnashala within few hours. Rama and Sita felt very happy to look beautiful hut. They appreciated for his hardwork and talent. After the slaughtering an animal, they entered the hut with utmost happiness. They later lived in it happily for few days.

CHAPTER THREE

One day Rama went to take bath in the river Godavari along with his wife. Laxmana also accompanied them. Laxmana told Rama, "Bharatha is doing a great penance. He forwent all the luxuries and living like a lay man for his mother's misdeeds. He who lived his luxuriously, now leading a very normal life like us" Rama felt very low for Bharatha's decision at the same time he felt very proud for having him as his brother. After they had taken bath, they went back to their hut.

After they had taken bath in the river, they went back to their hut. That day they spent happily in Panchavati with the hermits. Later Rama spent some time with Sita savouring beauty of the moon light at night. While they were in the conversation, a raakshasi came to the place. She is Shurpanka, the sister of Ravan. She saw the handsome Rama and craved for him with the feeling of lust. She also questioned Rama how he had come to their place with his wife.

Rama told everything and explained how he had come to the place. He also questioned her who she was. She also told everything about her. After that she told him that she had liked him very much and pleaded him to marry her. She warned Rama if he rejects her proposal, she would kill and eat his brother, Laxmana. She also told him to come along with her to her place and there they would enjoy, looking the beauty of nature.

Then Rama replied to lustful Shurpanka, "I am married and I love my wife. I don't agree with your proposal and make her sad with doing sinful things. My brother is unmarried and he is very handsome. He is suitable match to you. You can have him as your husband" On hearing the words of Rama, Shurpanka was convinced. She went to Laxmana and asked him to marry her.

Laxmana laughed at once on hearing her words. He said, "I am not suitable for you. Marry my brother, he is only the best husband for you. You can be second wife to him though he is married. He definitely leaves his old wife and marry you as you are looking fantastic. He loves you very much" Then Shurpanka went Rama again and asked him to marry her. She said that she would kill and eat Sita, later she would marry him. She also said that she would look Rama after very well in the forest.

Shurpanka next saw Sita with much anger and went to kill her. Then Laxmana came to Sita's rescue. He held a sharp sword and cut off her both ears and nose. Shurpanka was frightened and ran away to her place crying. She went to Khara, the leader of Raakshasas and complained him about the happening. Then Khara got angry on Rama and Laxmana. He immediately started to Panchavati to kill them for Laxmana's misdeed.

Before Khara started to Panchavati, he knew that his sister was hurt by Laxmana. His heart felt very sad after looking her pathetic condition. He promised Shurpanka that he would kill them and take revenge on them for hurting her. He described himself as a great being in the area and stated that no one would defeat him. Khara went with his fellow raakshasas who were very strong. They went Panchavati to attack on Rama and Laxmana.

When they went, Rama, Sita and Laxmana were taking rest in Parnashala. They suddenly came into the hut. Then Rama told Laxmana to take care of Sita meanwhile he would fight with them and send them away. Rama took his golden powerful bow and shot at them with powerful arrows. Khara challenged Rama that he will be defeated. Khara and his fellow raakshasas threw Shulas at them. Rama defended the shulas with his powerful arrows. And Rama immediately sent his numerous arrows at them. With them all the raakshasas fell onto the earth.

One of the raakshasas went to Khara and told him about the faintness of their fellows. Then Khara and the leader of his army, Dushanbe went toward Rama and Laxmana to directly fight with him. Along with them about fourteen thousands of raakshasas went to engage in the war. They were roaring like the thunders.

While they were moving the sounds of foxes trembled Khara. He suspected what it might be. He felt that something inauspicious things are going to be happened. But he did not go back. He darely resumed what they had felt earlier. On the other hand, Rama stood darely to fight with them. All the hermits and priests blessed him that he would win the war and slaughter them. Later Rama and Laxmana were surrounded by the raakshasas army as if it was sun's eclipse.

Later, the raakshasas threw all their Shulas at Rama and Laxmana. But without fear, Rama and Laxmana defended them with their powerful arrows. And in excess they used their arrows which made raakshasas terrified. They removed the armours of raakshasas. Thus Rama and Laxmana killed large number of raakshasas in the war. They were frightened at the skill of Rama and fled back to Khara to save them from him. Rama's the arrow of Gandharva terrified them.

Then Khara ordered his soldiers to countenance Rama as he was creating the horror. He ordered his army to kill him first so that they will be safe. Then their army went towards Rama. Khara's army threw thousands of arrows at Rama. Then Rama turned his bow in 360 degrees and shot powerful astras at them. With them all the raakshasas' armours fell onto the ground. Later the different astras killed their elephants and horses. The chariots and soldiers were sunk into the ground. The soldiers who were alive went to Khara to rescue them from Rama, the warrior.

The soldiers, who attacked on Rama, went to the Yama Loka. Then Dushana consoled them and prepared the other soldiers to fight with the two brothers. With the motivation of Dushana, the remaining soldiers went towards Rama to kill him. Then there was a terrible fight between Rama and raakshasas. All the raakshasas surrounded Rama. Doing nothing, it was inadundate for him to use Gandharva astra. When it was used the earth made terrible sound.

Later Dushana himself went towards Rama. Rama immediately killed his horses and cut off Dushana's hands which made him to fall onto the ground. Within few minutes Dushana and his army were succumbed to injuries made by Rama. Then Khara was very much angry with Rama. He took twelve giants along with him to fight with Rama. And Rama could easily kill them with his powerful weapons. Rama alone killed about fourteen thousands of soldiers in the war.

After Trisharasa had died, even Khara was terrified with the power of Rama. But he didn't hesitate to encounter him. Both fought ferociously in the war. Khara tried to break the bow of Rama with his sword. Khara even hurt Rama with his powerful weapons. Rama's armour fell onto the ground. Then Rama took his the bow of Vaishnava and used it against Khara. He shot his first arrow which made fell Khara's flag onto the ground. Later Rama destroyed their chariots, horses and elephants. That made Khara to stand on the ground. Then all the gods appeared from the heaven and blessed Rama for his heroic action in the war.

Khara boasted himself that he was a great warrior and ridiculed Rama for killing just normal raakshasas. Khara challenged Rama if he had dare enough to kill him. Then Khara threw his weapon, Gadha upon Rama. Rama simply defended that and it immediately smashed. Rama later threw many arrows which pricked in the body of Khara. The blood started pouring out like a stream. Later Rama burnt Khara's dead body with his arrow of fire. Thus Khara's episode was finished.

The gods from the heaven showered flowers on Rama for killing more than fourteen thousands of raakshasas. Lord Indra came to ashram where Rama was living in and appreciated Rama. Sita and Laxmana felt very proud of Rama.

One of the raakshasas who was not dead in the war, went to Lanka and told Ravana, "Oh! honourable king, our people were brutally killed in the war. Even our Khara was also killed" Then the ten headed Ravana was furious and raged. He angrily asked who he was. Ravana said, "How dare he? The ones who had done harm to me, wouldn't live anymore. Even the lord Indra and Yama has to face the music. I have the capacity of burning the sun" The raakshas told Ravana that it was Rama who killed their fellow raakshasas in the war.

Then Ravana felt that the gods might have sent Rama to kill our people. The raakshas told Ravana about Rama's skills at the war. He stated that our people would not stand before Rama. He also told Ravana about his brother, Laxmana. He was explaining Ravana how both the brothers engaged in war and killed their people. Then Ravana was raged and promised that he would kill both the brothers for killing his people.

Then the raakshas explained the greatness of Rama. He stated that no one would face him. That made him Ravana angry. Then the raakshas gave an idea of killing Rama. He told about his wife Sita, who is very beautiful. If she is abducted, Rama will definitely be died himself as he wouldn't live without her. Then Ravana was very happy with the idea of the raakshas.

Immediately Ravana started on his chariot to abduct Sita. On the way, he met Maricha. Maricha felicitated Ravana for coming to his place after a long time. Then they discussed about Rama and Ravana told his purpose of visiting the land. Ravana asked for the help to abduct Sita from the clutches of Rama. Then Maricha enquired how Ravana had got the idea of abducting Sita. Maricha objected his idea of abducting and suggested to look after his wives instead of doing this sinful thing.

CHAPTER FOUR

After Maricha had suggested Ravana not to abduct Sita, Ravana went back to Lanka. But Shurpanka went to Lanka and she provoked her brother to abduct Sita. Shurpanka was very furious about the deaths of their fellows and about her humiliation made by the two brothers. She explained Ravana about his greatness. She questioned him why he wouldn't kill abduct Sita. She reminded his conquers over the gods. But Ravana did not move with her words.

Then Shurpanka got angry on her brother, Ravana. She started scolding him for his attitude towards his people. She questioned why he remained silent while his people are dying in huge numbers. She stated that he was inefficient king to his people. A king should stand for the people. He shouldn't hesitate to take revenge on his enemies. She explained the greatness of Rama and how he is fulfilling the duties alloted by the gods. Why her brother was not like Rama and he had not the qualities as Rama had. She was trying to provoke her brother and wanted to commit sin that is abducting Sita from the clutches of Rama. And she wanted to take revenge on the two brothers for humiliating her.

Ravana asked Shurpanka, "Who is Rama? How much strength he has? What is his weapon?"

Shurpanka told, "Rama is the son of king, Dasharatha. He is

now in the exile for fourteen years due to fulfil his father's promise. He is a very good warrior. He alone killed fourteen thousands of people. Now he became the hero for the hermits in the forest. He has a beautiful wife and her name is Sita. She is suitable to you. Marry her so that your reputation will grow up. Rama's brother, Laxmana took off my clothes with force. The two brothers insulted me. So take revenge on them for ridiculed and teased your sister"

Ravana then was convinced with his sister's words and decided to take revenge on Rama for teasing his sister and killed his soldiers in huge number. Later he started to the place where Maricha lives in. Maricha again welcomes him and gave good accommodation. Later he enquired his purpose of coming to him. Ravana completely explained what had happened to his army and his sister, Shurpanka. Later, Ravana asked for Maricha's help for abducting Sita. Maricha asked how he could help him. Then Ravana told him to be in disguise of golden deer and saunter before Sita so that she would feel that you are the real deer. Then she craves for the deer and her husband will follow the deer. At that moment, I will disguise as a beggar and go for alms to their hut. When Sita come out, I will abduct her. Ravana's plan made Maricha shock. Maricha felt that it would not be good to be a part of the crime.

Maricha requested Ravana not to abduct Sita. He opined that Rama is a very good person. If we do that, he will also kill us. Rama is the form of righteousness. If we withdraw our plan, we will be saved. If you want to take revenge, fight with Rama but not the abduction of Sita.

Ravana objected the option of Maricha. He ordered just to follow what he had said. He ordered Maricha to disguise as the golden deer and stimulate Sita so that Rama will follow you. If you succeed in that, I will give you half of my kingdom. Without war, I will kill Rama, said Ravana.

Doing nothing, Maricha disguised himself as the golden deer. Ravana had shown the hut of Rama. He asked him to go and stand there. As Ravana said, Maricha started roaming in front of Parnashala. At the time, Sita was plucking flowers for her puja. Then Maricha went towards Sita and stood there until Sita sees him. After some time, Sita's eyes had fallen on the the golden deer. She was very much surprised to look at the deer.

Laxmana observed the scene and called her into the hut. Then Sita told, "See! "The beautiful golden deer" I want that" Then Laxmana told that it was a Black magic made by the raakshasas. He also told her that it was not a real deer. But Sita didn't listen to him. At anyhow, "I need that", Sita said. Since Sita wanted it, Rama called Jatayu and told him to look after Sita until he returns. "I will go and kill it with my arrow", said Rama. Rama also order Laxmana to take care of Sita and do not go anywhere leaving her alone in the hut. Laxmana said, "Ok"

Then Rama took his bow and arrows and went in the direction of the deer. The deer started its magic. It sometimes is appearing to him, sometimes not. When it appeared to him, he with utmost concentration shot at the deer. With the shot, the deer fell onto the ground as the powerful arrows were pierced into its body. Then the deer cried Sita! Laxmana! It was crying like Rama. When it was dead, it was looking like a giant. Then Rama understood that it was somebody's plot against them. Rama recollected

Laxmana's word and he felt very sorry for not listening to him. Rama thought that Sita and Laxmana feel that it was his sound. Then he rushed to the hut with its meat.

Sita heard the voice of her husband and she thought something had happened to her husband. She immediately ordered Laxmana to check if it was Rama. "If he is in the danger, go and save him", said Sita. But Laxmana said that his brother had ordered him not to leave his wife at any situation. So he said that he wouldn't go anywhere and he opined that was the magic voice made like his brother. Sita was very furious on Laxmana. She questioned if he was interested to see his brother's mishap. When Sita cried for Rama, Laxmana tried to move into the forest to save his brother.

But Laxmana had confidence that Rama is not in danger. But he worried about Sita for listening to his words. Sita was not listening to him. So, Laxmana decided to go but on one condition. He said that he would draw up a line, even at unavoidable circumstances, she would not cross it. Sita agreed for that and went into the forest in search of Rama.

After Laxmana had gone, Ravana appeared at the place. He laughed, everything was going as he planned. He was ready to use the situation to his advantage. Then Ravana was disguised as a priest and called Sita for alms. When she came out he was appreciating her beauty but Sita did not move. Ravana continued that Sita was attracting him and exclaimed that he had not seen such beauty in his life. He told that she shouldn't be in the forest but should be with him in the palace. Since Sita thought he was a priest, she treated him as her guest. She knew, "The guest is god" Then Ravana tried to abduct her. But Sita was looking into the forest if Laxmana was coming along with her husband.

Sita was frightened by Ravana's teasing words. He was continuously bullying her. Then Sita asked what his gothram was and if he was really a brahmin. She opined, a real brahmin never teases a woman. Then Ravana introduced himself to be a great king of Lankha. Ravana told that he started loving her at the very first sight. He said, "After seeing you, I started hating my wives and my love on them disappeared. Your beauty is equal to the beauty of five thousand women. So you can come with me and be as my wife. You will be treated as my dear wife in the palace.

Then Sita was angry with Ravana. She told him that she was the wife of the great Rama. My husband is equal to Lord Indra. My husband is a lion and you are a fox. There is a lot of difference between my husband and you. If you crave for me, it will be like putting your hand in the snake's mouth and jumping into the ocean tying a big rock to the waist. Then Ravana laughed loudly and started explaining the greatness of him. He said that the Kubera was his brother. Sita warned him it was okay touching the wife of Lord Indra but if he touched the wife of Rama, he will be turned into ashes.

Ravana asked Sita to come out of threshold and give him alms. Sita rejected his proposal. He said that when a priest comes to your house, will you send him without offering alms? He said that it would be a sin. Then Sita tried to come out of the line, drawn by Laxmana. But she suddenly recollected Laxmana's words. She rejected to come out. When Ravana tried to go inside, the sudden fire from the line, drawn by Laxmana came out. Ravana was afraid to look at the fire.

Then Ravana was very angry with Sita's behaviour. He forced her to come out and to perform alms. Then Sita thought that it would not be nice to send him without giving alms. As soon as Sita crossed the line, Ravana changed into his original form. Sita was frightened to look his giant form and ten big heads. Then he came forward and touched the thigh of Sita. He called for his chariot and it appeared before them. Immediately he dragged Sita into it. Then Sita started shouting to save her. Meanwhile the chariot flew into the air. Sita called Rama! Laxmana! Ravana is abducting me, "Save me" cried Sita. Ravana was laughing as his plan was successful and he told Sita that she must face the music as her husband's had done a great damage to them.

Sita did not notice anyone on their way. So she told the river Godavari to tell her husband about the abduction. Jatayu heard the cries of Sita and he flew up to the chariot. Sita saw Jatayu and felt very happy. She thought she would be saved by Jatayu.

Jatayu told Ravana that it would be a sin to abduct Sita who is the wife of Rama. He suggested Ravana to leave Sita immediately and act according to the righteousness. He told that Sita was in the form godess Laxmi. But Ravana made a deaf ear. Jatayu's words did not reach into his ears. Ravana laughed at Jatayu and said to him that he was not going to leave her. Then Jatayu told him if he was not ready to leave her, he would be going to face consequences. Ravana told with pride that no one would conquer him and he declared himself to be the greater than trinity.

Jatayu challenged Ravana to win over him and take Sita. He said, "Though I am very old and you are young, I am ready to fight with you to save Sita. While I am alive and I would not let you take Sita" Then Ravana agreed to fight with Jatayu. Though Jatayu was a small creature before Ravana, he fought bravely with him. Jatayu defended all the arrows of Ravana and spoiled his chariot and pierced with his beak all over his body. Jatayu also killed the donkeys which were driving the chariot.

CHAPTER FIVE

Later Ravana and Sita had fallen onto the ground. Ravana got furious on Jatayu and he took his sharp sword from his dagger and cut off Jatayu's wings at once. With that Jatayu had fallen onto the ground and died later. Sita then started crying loudly looking at the dead body of Jatayu. She blamed herself because Jatayu had died because of her. Sita started calling Rama! Rama! Then Ravana held her hair tightly and started his journey to Lanka. With that awful thing, the light had disappeared and the hermits felt very sad for this untoward happening. They also felt Ravana's death was about happen. Meanwhile Ravana flew into the sky, holding Sita.

Sita blamed Ravana while he was taking her away from her husband. She treated him as a human animal. She pointed her finger at him and said in a solemn voice; "If my husband was present there, you would become a corpse" She also reminded Ravana that her husband alone killed Ravana's fourteen thousand soldiers for attacking her husband. She warned him lastly to leave her at that moment otherwise he must face the consequence but Ravana did not care her words.

Sita couldn't do anything. She was trying to let loose herself from the clutches of Ravana but he held her firmly. So she gave up. When they were flying, Sita saw five monkey men in the forest. So she dropped her jewels before the monkey men without being noticed by Ravana.

The money men saw Ravana abducting Sita. They felt very sad meanwhile Ravana crossed the sea and entered Lanka. He kept her in a private palace and ordered the raakshasas to look after her.

Ravana also told raakshasas to give whatever Sita asks. Then he thought of killing Rama so that his enmity will be fulfilled. For that he sent eight raakshasas to kill Rama. After killing Rama, Ravana thought of marrying Sita. Later Ravana asked to fulfil his lust but Sita sat among the raakshasas and started crying. Then he boasted about himself and his wealth. He forcefully showed his palace. Though he boasted himself and offered the queenship of Lanka, Sita simply rejected his proposal.

Then Sita started telling the greatness of her husband. She simply stated that Ravana was lesser than Rama in every aspect and more Rama had a good character. And he never looked at the others' wives with the desire of lust. She also talked about the greatness of Laxmana. "If they know about my abduction, they can kill you", said Sita. She also warned him that he was going to die soon. Ravana laughed at her mock warnings. He told Sita that he was giving her a chance to think about his proposal for a year. "After that I will not see you talking like this", said Ravana. He also ordered the female raakshasas to torture her until she accepts with his proposal.

So the raakshasas took her to Ashoka garden. There Sita was imprisoned. They were daily torturing Sita. Sita bore everything but she did not surrender to them. Every day she was crying for Rama.

Lord Indra came to know about the abduction of Sita by Ravana. He felt very sad for that. Indra immediately went to Lord Brahma and told about the incident. He told Brahma Sita had been abducted for the welfare of the hermits and to kill the raakshasas but Sita was crying continuously without having food and water. She was worrying about her husband and waiting that he would take her back. "If she continues that, she will die", said Indra.

Then Lord Brahma responded positively and promised that he would take care of Sita. Brahma told Indra that Rama would go to Lanka and kill Ravana. Then Indra felt very happy. But he questioned how Sita would live without eating. Brahma then gave him ambrosia and told him to give it to Sita.
Indra went to Lanka in disguise and offered ambrosia to Sita. Sita at first did not recognize him but after Indra had shown his original form, she took and had ambrosia. Indra told her that Rama and Laxmana would definitely come and take you back after killing Ravana.

Sita was very happy to know the details of Rama and Laxmana. She requested Indra to be helpful to her husband and his brother. Indra promised her that he would be with him at every situation. Sita felt very happy with Indra's promise. Later Sita got confidence and stopped crying. Indra took leave from Sita and went to Indraloka. The raakshasas surprised to see the sudden change in Sita.

Rama on the other hand went into the deep forest to kill the golden deer. There he noticed that it was not a deer but it was Maricha who deliberately came in disguise. He killed Maricha with his arrows and started coming back to his Parnashala. On the way, he heard cries of foxes. He felt that something had happened to Sita. He also heard Maricha crying like him while dying. While Rama was returning, he came across his brother who was coming hurriedly for Rama. Rama asked Laxmana why he had left Sita alone in the hut. "I feel this is an inauspicious time and the raakshasas may cause trouble to Sita", said Rama.

Rama thus worried about Sita if Sita had been in a trouble. Later Rama and Laxmana rushed to Parnasala and they were astonished to find the absence of Sita in the hut. Rama blamed Laxmana for leaving his wife alone though he instructed not to leave her alone. Rama broke into tears and felt very sad. He couldn't bear the situation. His loving wife's absence in the hut made him bore the brunt. He was crying continuously.

Rama asked repeatedly Laxmana why he had left Sita alone in Parnasala. Then Laxmana told his brother that Sita herself had pleaded him to go into forest to save her husband. "Even I heard the voice you. It said that you are in a danger. Sita continuously provoked me to come to save you in the forest. I told her that no one would do harm or kill you but with a lot of love on you, she pleaded me to save you. So it has become inevitable situation for me. When I rejected to go, she blamed me that I was looking for the death you. Since she suspected me, I came into the forest" Laxmana told Rama.

Then Rama questioned Laxmana how he would simply care the words of a lady without looking her protection. Then where his words had gone to take care of her before entering the forest to kill the deer?

Finally they let the topic go. Rama told "Whatever had

happened had happened; now there was no use of talking. Let's look for Sita. Where had she gone? What happened to her? Did anyone do harm to her? Let's go and ask anyone who are on the way or else we can ask the trees and the rivers about her", Rama said to Laxmana.

They searched for Sita but did not find the evidence of Sita. They looked in all the directions. They asked the trees and the river Godavari but no use. Nobody replied to them. Rama cried as there was no reply from anyone. He felt what he would tell her father when he asks about his daughter. Laxaman went in the direction of South as the animals were looking at the south. Rama also followed Laxmana in that direction. After they had travelled for several miles, they saw the flowers on the ground. Rama recognized the flowers which were usually worn by his wife, Sita. So Rama asked the hills and brooks whether they had seen his wife.

Then the hills told him that two people fought each other for a lady. "We don't whether she was Sita", they said. They had shown the evidences of the fight. Rama saw the remnants of bow and other weapons. He also saw the dead bodies of donkeys. Rama cried that the raakshasas took revenge on him by abducting Sita. Rama pleaded the gods to tell the information about his wife otherwise he would smash the whole world. "If they give back his wife, he can kill all the raakshasas", said Rama. Rama raged and his eyes turned into red. He is looking as lord Rudra.

Then Laxmana tried to appease him. He prostrated not to get furious. He told that Rama was conquered over his all senses. It would not be fine to show his anger which will cause damage to the society. He, who has to protect the world, will not cause damage. So Laxmana appeased with his words. "It is not that we should spoil the world, it is the time to search for Sita", said Laxmana. He requested Rama to behave well.

Rama was appeased with soothing words of Laxmana. He felt that it was good to be with patience. He decided to search for Sita but he doesn't know where and how to search. He asked his brother, "How can we find Sita?" With that Laxmana thought for a while and came with an idea that they would go in the same direction as they found some evidences. After they had travelled for some more miles, they found Jatayu, lying on the ground. Laxmana thought that Jatayu might have killed Sita and he immediately was about to shoot it. Just then, he found, Jatayu shedding blood.

On seeing Rama, Jatayu told that Ravana had abducted Sita. He told that he had tried his level best to let loose Sita but Ravana cut off his wings. Then Laxmana felt very sad for thinking badly about Jatayu and he started crying. Rama went to Jatayu and hugged him. Rama felt miserable for the troubles he had continuously. Rama and Laxmana felt unhappy for his father's friend's pathetic condition.

Seeing Jatayu, Rama spoke with Laxmana in this way, "This Jayatu has fought for me. Though his strength is less, he fought with the strong Ravana. I really pity on him" Rama asked Jatayu about Sita and what had happened to her. How did Ravana steal her? What harm did I do to him? He asked several questions about Sita and Ravana. Then Jatayu opened his mouth and told Rama everything, how Ravana abducted and how he cut off his wings. Jatayu also told Rama not to worry about Sita. She will come back after Ravana will be killed by you. He told Rama that Ravana was the brother of Kubota. While Jatayu was speaking, he vomited the blood and died later.

CHAPTER SIX

Rama cried looking the corpse of Jatayu. He has been living in the forest for a long time. And he died today because of Rama. Jatayu from then was worshipped as he aided Sita. Rama ordered Laxmana to bring the dried wood for pyre. They placed Jatayu on the pyre and did his cremation according to the rituals. Later Rama and Laxmana prayed for his soul may take rest in peace in the heaven. Later they took bath in the Godavari and started travelling further in search of Sita.

They went into deeper of the forest. They crossed many ashrams and encountered many cruel animals. They found a hill in the middle of the forest and it had a cave. They entered the cave and there they saw a giant. The giant terrified them with its wicked body. It ridiculed Laxmana which made him raged. Laxmana went to him and cut off his ears and nose with his sharp sword.

Laxmana suggested Rama to be careful as his left arm was shaking. Meanwhile the terrible sound terrified them. His hands are very long and had an eye in the stomach. To their surprise, he had no head. He was simply sitting in the giant chair and dragging animals and keeping them in his stomach. Laxmana was afraid to look at him. Then Rama soothed him not to afraid of the giant. The giant introduced himself. He said that he was Kabandha. He said not to afraid of him. He told Rama if he is buried by Rama, they would get the power of sixth sense.

Rama and Laxmana buried and cremated him and Kabandha immediately changed into Gandharva. Kabandha once was Gandharva because of the curse, he turned into the giant. That day his curse was gotten redemption by Rama. As Rama helped him, Gandharva told to make friendship with Sugreeva. "Sugreeva will be helpful to you in searching Sita", said Gandharva.

Kabandha who is now Gandharva told Rama that there was a river called Pampa. You go there and leave your misery at the bank of the river. One more thing is Sabari, an old lady has been waiting for you for a long time. After seeing you, she will join the heaven choir. From there, you can go to the hill, Rishyamukha. The hill contained a cave which was covered with rocks. In the cave, Sugreeva, Vanara king is residing. Go and meet him. Make friendship with him as he is a very nice and humble. He will be helpful to you in searching Sita. Later Gandharva flew to the heaven.

As Gandharva said, Rama and Laxmana started their journey towards the river, Pampa. They reached Sabari ashram and took blessings of her. Sabari was on cloud nine, looking Rama. She gave them a nice accommodation and hospitality. Sabari asked the welfare of Rama and shot at him plenty of questions. Sabari was very happy to see him in her ashram.

Sabari later adored Rama with much devotion. She spent some time with Rama and Laxmana. Later she slept in the lap of Rama and changed as the light form. That light went to the heaven. After Sabari had demised, Rama told Laxmana, "We are very grateful to be here and experienced wonderful memories with Sabari" They later started their journey towards Rushyamukha Hill.

Rama and Laxmana reached the river Pampa and surprised to look at the beauty of the surroundings but his sadness was haunting him. He told Laxmana that he had been suffering due to Kaikeyi. She sent him and his wife to the forest. "Now she is abducted which made me very unhappy. But the place subsided my sadness a little. The hills, flowers and birds are looking so fantastic", said Rama.

Then the king of Vanara, Sugreeva was sauntering in the area. He saw Rama and Laxmana and surprised. He didn't know who they were. He felt that they were aliens. He thought that they will do harm to them. He immediately went back to his place and there he told to his ministers that the enemies sent by Vali were roaming in their area. He also told them that they came in disguise to smash their kingdom. Then the ministers decided to go to Rama and Laxmana to know who they were.

After some time, the minsters went to the place where Rama and Laxmana were staying. They were afraid of Rama and Laxmana as they might be the men of Vali. Then one of Sugreeva's ministers, Hanuman told them that they were not the men of Vali. So don't afraid of Vali, he won't do anything, said Hanuman. The people of Vali do not contain the long arms and legs. They are looking like very clever men. Then Sugreeva ordered Hanuman to go to them and enquire who they were. Then Hanuman decided to converse with Rama and Laxmana.

Before Hanuman went to meet Rama and Laxmana, he had changed into the form of a saint. Hanuman went to then and at first he introduced himself. Later he asked them who they were. Hanuman also asked them where they had come from. "The animals are roaming here. Are you not afraid of them?" asked Hanuman.

Though Hanuman was asking them questions repeatedly, Rama and Laxmana did not utter a word and they looked Hanuman in surprise. Then Hanuman told about Sugreeva that his brother, Vali had done harm to him. Now Sugreeva was roaming in the forest with the grief. "Sugreeva sent me here to know about you. I am Hanuman, his minister. My father is the god of wind. Since Sugreeva requested me, I came in the form of the saint. I came from the hill of Rushyamukha" said Hanuman.

Then Rama felt very happy and he introduced himself and his brother to Hanuman. Then Hanuman engaged in conversation with them which made Rama very happy. Rama also surprised with the oratory, fluency and accuracy of the language of Hanuman. Hanuman knew all the vedas which made Rama and Laxmana astonish. Rama stated that Sugreeva was very fortunate to have Hanuman as his minister. Such ministers can perform any difficult activity with much ease.

Then Laxmana spoke with Hanuman in this way, "Hanuman, the scholor! We are also looking for Sugreeva. We will be helpful to him" Hanuman was elated with the words of Laxmana. Then he decided to unite Rama and Sugreeva.

Later Hanuman took Rama and Sita to Sugreeva. He felt that Sugreeva would get back his kingdom definitely. While they were traveling Hanuman asked them how they had come to the dense forest. Then Rama told Laxmana to explain their story to Hanuman.

Then Laxmana spoke with Hanuman in this way, "Dasharatha, the king of Ayodhya was our father. He was ruling the country fairly. All the people were very happy with his rule. Rama is the elder son and I am Rama's younger brother. Rama is the most truthful and righteousness in the world. He looks after all the living beings on the earth. He didn't even care the kinghood for the sake of our father's promise. Now we are in the exile for fourteen years. During our exile my brother's wife, Sita was abducted by Ravana. Kabandha told us that Sugreeva would help us in finding Sita. So we came here to meet Sugreeva"

Then Hanuman felt sad by knowing their pathetic story. He thought, "Great people came to take the help of my king, Sugreeva. Every has to take the help of Rama but now he is in the need. How fate decided like this? Sugreeva is very lucky for being helpful to Rama" Hanuman shed tears for Rama's situation.

"The great people like you came for Sugreeva. He will definitely help you. He is also in the need now. His brother, Vali abducted his wife. Now two brothers became enemies. You should help him in getting back his wife. We all search for Sita" said Hanuman.

Laxmana was very happy with Hanuman's kind heart. He told Rama that Hanuman became a part of us in searching

Sita. Hanuman doesn't speak lies and it seems he is honest man. Later Hanuman came into his original form that is Vanara and took them to Sugreeva.

They reached their cave where Sugreeva was sitting in his throne. Hanuman told everything about Rama and Laxmana. He also explained how Rama's had been abducted. "Now they came for your help in rescuing Sita. They came to know that Ravana had abducted her. These two brothers are equal to gods so we should adore and pray them", said Hanuman.

Then Sugreeva came down from the platform and held Rama's hand and embraced him as a friendly gesture. Then all the vanaras welcomed Rama and Laxmana into their cave on the flowers' path which is arranged by Hanuman. Rama accepted their hospitality and to make friendship with Sugreeva. They made Rama sit on the branch of grape fruit tree after it was cut off and another branch for Laxmana.

Sugreeva then started narrating his story to Rama. He said that he had been sauntering in the forest with the threat my elder brother. "Vali had abducted my wife, unable to encounter him, I had hidden myself in this cave. So please help in getting back my wife" Sugreeva said.

Then Rama smiled at him and promised that he would kill Vali for abducting your wife. With my powerful weapons, I will kill him so do not worry. Then Sugreeva felt very happy for soothing words of Rama. Hanuman felt very happy for Rama and Sugreeva. As he wanted, both became friends.

Sugreeva was elated to hear the words of Rama. He saluted Rama with reverence. Later Sugreeva promised that he had not known anything about Ravana. "Even I did not know where he lived, what religion he belonged to. He also requested Rama to subside his grief for Sita. He had a hope that he would definitely kill Ravana and get back Sita. So be with dareness. Even I am in the same situation but didn't get disheartened. I will be helpful to you. Let's together take revenge on our enemies" said Sugreeva.

Thus Sugreeva consoled Rama and Rama could get back to normalcy. Rama felt that Sugreeva could play the role of a friend. He knew friend's role is very important in everyone's life. So Rama felt very lucky to have Sugreeva as his friend. Rama told that he would be helpful to him and in the same way Sugreeva would be helpful to him. Rama assured him that he will not speak lies and he had not spoken before and ever. Everyone knows that he is the man of truthful and righteousness.

Later Sugreeva spoke with Rama in this way, "Hanuman has told me that you are in exile for fourteen years and you have also worried about your wife. I will definitely help you in retrieving her. She might be anywhere in the world or above the world or beneath the world. It is the duty of me to take her back. I had a suspicious that I saw a lady few days back, she might be Sita. That lady was crying Rama and Laxmana repeatedly. She dropped her jewels while somebody was taking her in the sky. I collected those jewels and kept them safely"

Them Rama asked to show him the jewels with much eagerness. Sugreeva went into his cave immediately and got them back and shown to Rama. Rama identified Utharabaranam and he exclaimed that it belonged to his wife. He cried at once on seeing the jewel. And Laxmana identified her anklets and rings. "Oh! It must be Ravana who took Sita", said Laxmana.

Rama asked Sugreeva to give the information about Ravana. He also asked in which direction they went. Where that person lived but Sugreeva told that he had known anything about Ravana. Sugreeva felt very sad for not giving information which Rama asked.

Later Sugreeva cut off another branch which has full of beautiful flowers. They sat on the branch and Hanuman sat on the other branch. Then Sugreeva wanted to share something with Rama. Rama knew that Sugreeva wanted to speak with him. He asked Sugreeva to speak freely with him.

Sugreeva said, "My brother is threatening me. I have life threat from him. So I have hidden myself in the cave. He has abducted my wife. So please save me from him and see that my wife will be free from him. You are my friend and my enemy is your enemy" Rama then was convinced with the explanation of Sugreeva and he promised him that he would kill his brother with his arrows.

Sugreeva felt very happy with the reply of Rama and he continued in this way, "My brother kicked out me from the kingdom and stole my wife. He has been waiting for the chance to kill me. These vanaras are protecting me in the forest. If my brother dies, I will be very happy. We are also happy "

Rama told him that feel that his enemy had died. Once I gave an assurance, no one would prevent that. I have the ability to kill Vali. Then Sugreeva got the courage and he felt that his grandeur life will be revived. And Sugreeva was ready to fight with his brother, Vali.

Sugreeva observed Rama and told him, "Rama! You should kill my brother with your bow and arrows. I will be very happy" Rama then embraced Sugreeva and suggested him to make a move to Kishkinda later he would follow them. And there you invite Vali to the war. Meanwhile we come there and hide behind the trees, said Rama.

As said by Rama, Sugreeva went to Kishkinda and called Vali to the war. Vali with anger participated in the war. The two brothers fought ferociously. Rama on the other hand, wore his bow and observing their fight. While they were fighting, Rama couldn't identify Vali as they both looked alike. So he didn't shoot the arrow.

After some time, Sugreeva was unable bear Vali's strength,

ran away into his house. Vali beat him black and blue. Vali left his brother without killing him. After that Rama and Laxmana went to Sugreeva. Sugreeva felt ashamed of himself. And he asked Rama why he had not killed his brother, Vali.

Rama said to him not to get anger. He said that he couldn't identify who is who as both were looking alike. Then Rama told him to again fight with Vali but this time he had to wear the garland so that he could identify him. Sugreeva agreed with the proposal of Rama. He wore the garland and went to Vali again. Vali again came out his palace and started fighting with Sugreeva.

For few hours, the terrible fight had been occurred between Vali and Sugreeva. Again Vali was becoming very strong and beating Sugreeva like anything. Then Rama shot an arrow at Vali which straight away pierced in the heart of Vali. With that Vali fell onto the ground at once and later went into unconscious state. Then Rama went to Vali and he noticed that Vali was at the edge of death. Vali opened eyes and told Rama, "Do you feel that it is your greatness to kill from behind? You are a man with good qualities. Is it good to backstabbing? Vali asked adamantly why Rama had done like that?"

Srirama started giving explanation to Vali for killing him from the backside. "You are blaming me in anger. I have killed you for not standing on the righteousness. You have abducted your brother's wife who is equal to sister. That was a sin. So you have been punished in this way. Being a Kshathriya, I can't bear your sin. Sugreeva is like my brother as Laxmana. We kill wild animals which are cruel and you have also behaved like an animal so I killed you"

Vali reciprocated in this way, "I ask my apologies for behaving so. I have a son named Angadha. Please protect him. I fought with my Sugreeva and it is going to be ended with my death" Rama then consoled him not to worry about the mistake he committed. This act will sweep all of your sins. Now you will join the heaven choir. I will protect Angadha. Do not worry about him. While they were speaking, Vali closed his eyes and slept permanently. Angadha came and broke into tears at his father's body.

Later Hanuman preached Vedantha to Tara who is wife of Vali. Tara told that she would follow her husband. She later killed herself, unable bear her husband's death. With much grief all of them cremated their bodies according to traditions.

After that Rama and others went to Sugreeva who was in the grief and consoled him. Hanuman and other Vanaras saluted Rama with respect for getting back their kingdom which had been in hands of Vali over the years. Rama ordered them to make Angadha as their prince. They then requested him come into their kingdom but Rama rejected their proposal as he was in the forest exile for fourteen years. In few more my exile will be completed.

Rama continued, "In the month of Karthika, you should help me in killing Ravana. Meanwhile you enter your kingdom and rule it, leading your life luxuriously. This is our united promise. Stand on it"

Later Sugreeva entered his kingdom with his vanaras. And they did his coronation as a king and Angadha as their prince. Ruma, Sugreeva's wife became the queen of Kishkinda.

After Sugreeva had been done coronation, Rama and Laxmana decided to stay in the same cave in Rushymuka hill where Sugreeva and his army lived in. After going into the cave, Rama spoke with Laxmana in this way, "This cave is so wide and well ventilated. We should stay here until the monsoon completes. The place is nice to live in but I am more worried about Sita. That night Rama couldn't sleep as Sita's memories were haunting him. Laxmana tried to console him but it went in futile. They both thought how they would know about Ravana. How they would get back Sita. Laxmana told that Sugreeva would try to find Ravana meanwhile we would be very patient for four months.

Sugreeva on the other hand was enjoying his life in the kingdom. He was on different pilgrimage with his wife. He handed over all his duties to his ministers. And Hanuman especially was taking care of everything. He and his people were on cloud nine.

Hanuman told, "We are happy because of Rama. We should not forget his help. So it is our duty to search Sita. We have about one crore of soldiers. We should send them in different directions to search her. Our time of four months came to end in three days. If we don't search, we will be given death punishment by Rama"

So Hanuman ordered his soldiers to go and search her all over the world.

Sugreeva went to Neeludu who had one crore of soldiers. He wanted to take his help in identifying Sita. Neela and his soldiers started searching Sita.

CHAPTER EIGHT

Rama on the other hand felt dejected. He felt four months to be four years. Laxmana found his desperation in his brother. He also could do nothing but to console him. Then Rama told his brother, "Sugreeva forgot his duty. He took my help but forgot to help me. So you go to Sugreeva's kingdom and order him that I was very angry with him.

Laxmana went to Kishkinda and met Sugreeva. He had shown very much anger on Sugreeva. With his red face, he warned Sugreeva and asked him if he wanted to be killed as his brother by Rama. He asked him why he had forgotten his task. Even Angadha also told his uncle that Rama was angry on him. But Sugreeva did not respond to them. Then the vanaras came and played the music. With that music he came out of the sleep. Then he came to know that Laxmana had come to meet him and they also told that Rama was very angry on him for neglecting.

Sugreeva then understood Laxmana's rage after he was told by Angadha and the ministers. He was surprised why Laxmana was angry with him. He didn't understand what mistake had been done by him. Then Hanuman recalled his promise to Rama. He told that he had completely forgotten searching Sita. The given time was over but we didn't try for it. Rama was also angry with him as he had done mistake. Go and ask apology to Laxmana otherwise we will be killed.

Meanwhile Laxmana entered the room where Sugreeva was taking rest. He was terrified with Laxmana. Tara and Ruma came to Sugreeva's rescue. They pleaded Laxmana to appease. Then Laxmana reminded his task. Then Sugreeva told that he had started searching for Sita. He told that he had sent Neela's army for the task.

Sugreeva asked his apology to Laxmana. On knowing the truth, Laxmana was appeased. Then Sugreeva became free from fear. He told that he had gotten his kingdom due to Rama. How he would forget his duty so simply. I would only help him in identifying Ravana's place. Rama himself has to kill Ravana and get back Sita. Sugreeva repented for his mistake and said sorry.

Then Laxmana told, "You know Rama is a man of righteousness. I am unable to console him being a brother. He was gloomy with the loss of his wife. So let's do something for him"

Sugreeva ordered Hanuman to bring all of his army to the kingdom. Within ten days we should try to find out Sita. We have the army of crores. Everyone should perform their duty. It is his order otherwise death punishment will be imposed who neglects his duty. Hanuman immediately went and told the news to all the vanaras. They all rushed to the kingdom and stood before Sugreeva. Sugreeva felt very happy. They came with several gifts but he rejected all of them. He told that they needed Sita's appearance. They immediately went for searching Sita.

Sugreeva later went with Laxmana to meet Rama. On seeing Rama, he fell on his feet, asking apology. Rama felt very happy on seeing his army who came for searching his wife. Then Rama embraced Sugreeva with friendly gesture. Rama told that the time for war is approaching. Sugreeva told Rama that his men would go and get Sita back after killing Ravana. Rama felt very happy with the words of Sugreeva.

Rama thanked Sugreeva for helping him in identifying Sita. He said, "Its like the sun has risen in my life. I am very fortunate to have you as my friend. I will conquer anyone if you stand by my side. Ravana abducted Sita for his downfall. I will kill him with my sharp arrows soon" Meanwhile crores of vanaras came and stood before Sugreeva. They were waiting for his order.

Sugreeva said to Rama, "With your permission, I will send vanaras for the task" Rama replied that as it was hid army, he told to Sugreeva to order them. He told that he wanted to know Sita soon. Firstly Sugreeva sent one lakh vanaras to the east in search of Sita. He gave them a month time. If they don't come in time, they will be given death punishment.

Later he sent Neeludu, Hanuman, Jamba antha and others to the south direction. The team was headed by Angadha. And he sent his uncle and others to the west.

Sugreeva at last sent Shathabali and the team to the North. He ordered them to search for her every nook and corner of the world. After few days the teams from the west and north came and said that they had not found Sita anywhere. And the team from the east told the same. So they came to conclusion that Sita had been taken towards south. So it was possible for Hanuman to take her back.

Hanuman and the other vanaras went in the direction of the south but they didn't find Sita anywhere. They didn't stop searching for her. They were eating fruits and stems and proceeding further. They even into the deepest of forest where they were no animals. There they found Kandu Maharshi, who had a lot of anger. Since the Maharshi lost his son who was just ten years old, he cursed the forest.

The vanaras team went into the cave but they did not see Sita there. They saw a raakshasa who was like a big hill. He saw the vanaras and tried to attack them. Then Angadha beat him with his palm, with that the raakshasa fell onto the ground, vomiting the blood. They found another cave and they also went into cave. Even there, they didn't see Sita.

The vanaras spoke eachother, "We searched for Sita everywhere but we couldn't find her. At least we could not find the evidence. If we don't find, Sugreeva will punish us so let's not dejected. We should have persistence now"

Then Angadha and the team went towards south again. They saw many hills but no use. They took rest under the trees and proceeding. They reached the mountain of Vindhya. They searched in the all caves of the mountain. Hanuman searched for her at every nook and corner.

There they found a cave which was guarded by a raakshasa. They saw the swans and other birds were coming out as there were plenty of fruits and flowers. They were coming out for their food. The vanaras were astonished to see a lady who wore the fabric clothes. Hanuman went to her and asked who she was.

Hanuman went to the lady and asked in this way, "We have exhausted and felt very thirsty. Whose is this golden tree? How beautiful the flowers are! How the golden tortoises are roaming!"

Then the lady replied to Hanuman, "Here sacred man lives here. He built this golden forest. His name is Mayavi. He had performed the great penance for that Lord Brahma appeared and gave him a boon. He lived happily for some years. Lord Indra told to kill him for showing his lust on Hema, who was a damsel. Later Indra gave this to Hema. I was born to Merusavarni. My name is Swayamprabha. Now I am looking after it" She asked Hanuman how they had come here. Before answering to her, she told them to have fruits and water.

CHAPTER NINE

Then all the vanaras had the fruits and water. Then their exhaust had disappeared. Hanuman started narrating their story. He told what had happened to Rama from Ayodhya episode to Sugreeva's episode. He told her that they had come here with the order of their king, Sugreeva. Then Swayamprabha was very happy with them. Hanuman requested her to save them as the given time by Sugreeva was over. So they requested her to send them back. Then Swayamprabha told them to close their eyes and they did so. She strictly told them not to open their eyes. When they closed their eyes, to their astonishment, they came out within a minute.

After Swayamprabha had gone, Vanaras crossed the forest and their they found a sea. It was roaring and rising with its wave. When they went there, the given time by Sugreeva was over. They felt very sad for not fulfilling their king's desire.

Angadha told the vanaras that they couldn't fulfil their task so it was better to die rather than going back. They decided kill themselves. But vanaras were afraid of Angadha's idea. But they knew that their king would kill them if they went without telling about Sita's news.

Tarudu was one of the vanaras told that they would live in the cave. Here plenty of fruits and stems are available. If we live here, no one could harm them. The other vanaras appreciated his idea.

Then Angadha started crying for his position. Then all the vanaras told that this was because of Sugreeva. He unnecessarily had given this task to us. They started praising Vali and cursing Sugreeva for keeping them in this position. When they were worrying, they suddenly heard a strange voice from the cave.

All the vanaras decided to kill themselves. Just then an eagle appeared before them. Its name was Sampathi, who was younger brother of Jatayu. It came from the cave. Seeing them, it asked vanaras, who were in grief. Then Hanuman told Sampathi, "We have come here in search of Sita. Our king, Sugreeva sent us to find her. We did not fulfil, given task. Rama was worrying about Sita for his wife's abduction. Jatayu also tried to save her but Ravana killed it. As we didn't succeed, we are killing ourselves"

Then Sampathi got angry as Jatayu was its brother. It asked, "Who was that cruel fellow? How dare he to kill my brother? It asked them all the details how and why had happened all the incident"

It said that its wings had been burnt due to the sun shine. So it was unable fly and hiding itself in the cave. Then Angadha went and took it down from the hill. He started narrating the whole story of Rama and Sita. Why they had been exiled. How Rama had killed the raakshasas. How Maricha disguised as the golden deer. How Jatayu tried to help Sita while Ravana was taking it away. He told it that Sita had dropped her jewels as the evidence for Rama.

Then Sampathi told that Ravana was the brother of Kubera. He lives in Lankha. When they asked about Lankha's address, it said that it was very far away. You have to cross the big sea. The sea was spread bout 1500 kilometers. If you cross it, you will find Lankha. There Sita was imprisoned in the garden of Ashoka. The raakshasas were guarding her. You can see Ravana also there. The vanaras were stupefied with the reply of Sampathi.

Sampathi asked them to take it near to the sea so that they could do its brother's rituals. They did so and it performed the rituals to its brother, Jatayu. At last vanaras felt very happy for knowing the secret of Sita. Sampathi also told them that its son, Suparswa had seen Ravana's abduction.

The vanaras discussed themselves that the news made them happy but who would cross the sea which was very broader and longer in size. They knew nobody could cross it and come back. They asked Jambavantha for the advice. Then Jambavantha told not be worry. He told that Hanuman could do the task easily. Jambavantha started telling the greatness of Hanuman. He opined that Hanuman had all the qualities. He was equal to Rama, Laxmana and Sugreeva. Apart from the physical strength, Hanuman was mentally strong.

Jambavantha started narrating Hanuman's childhood story. He was the son of the wind god. He told the adventures Hanuman had done during his childhood. Finally Jambavantha came to the conclusion that Hanuman was only the person to fly and cross the sea. All the vanaras started motivating Hanuman to fly. They clapped and praised to fly.

Hanuman then knew his power and at once he rose very big in size. His body expanded to hundred times bigger than the previous. He said, "I am the son of the wind god. I can cross the sea with my strength. I can break the earth and lift the hill. Suddenly he rose to the sky and the vanaras felt as if they were looking Vamana"

Hanuman then flew as the speed of wind. Within seconds he was in the sky and moving above the sky. All the vanaras were dumbfounded. The vanaras left their grief and in were surprise. They did not think that Hanuman could cross the sea. They bid him the grand farewell, telling that their lives would depend on him.

Hanuman started his journey in the sky like an aeroplane. He crossed the mountain of Mahendra. When he stepped on the hill, it roared with big voice. The animals on it were afraid of the sound. From there he started his journey to Lankha.